LEADERS OF
ANCIENT ROME

HADRIAN Consolidating
the Empire

LEADERS OF
ANCIENT ROME

HADRIAN

Consolidating
the Empire

Julian Morgan

the rosen publishing group's
rosen
central

Published in 2003 by The Rosen Publishing Group, Inc.
29 East 21st Street, New York, NY 10010

First Edition

Library of Congress Cataloging-in-Publication Data

Morgan, Julian, 1958–
Hadrian: consolidating the Empire / Julian Morgan.— 1st ed.
p. cm. — (Leaders of Ancient Rome)
Includes bibliographical references and index.
Summary: A biography of the Roman emperor and general who extended the empire's frontiers as far as England and brought Rome to the height of its power.
ISBN 0-8239-3593-0 (alk. paper: library binding)
1. Hadrian, Emperor of Rome, 76–138—Juvenile literature.
2. Emperors—Rome—Biography—Juvenile literature. 3. Rome—History—Hadrian, 117–138—Juvenile literature. [1. Hadrian, Emperor of Rome, 76–138. 2. Kings, queens, rulers, etc.
3. Rome—History—Hadrian, 117–138.] I. Title. II. Series.
DG295 .M67 2002
937'.07'092—dc21

2001005399

Manufactured in the United States of America

CONTENTS

ITALY AT THE TIME OF HADRIAN

• Luca

ETRURIA

ITALIA

Roma

• Tusculum

Astura •

• Arpinum

Formiae •

Via Appia

• Puteoli

SARDINIA

MEDITERRANEAN SEA

Lilybaeum •

SICILIA

• Syracusae

PATH TO POWER

CHAPTER 1

2
3
4
5

On August 11, AD 117, at the age of forty-one, Publius Aelius Hadrianus, governor of Syria, became emperor of Rome. It was a momentous time for the Roman Empire, especially after the popular campaigns and military expansions of the previous emperor, Trajan, who had just died in Selinus, Cilicia. Hadrian's first task was to confirm himself in his new role by receiving the acceptance of others, something he could in no way have taken for granted at that time.

Trajan had been on his way home, worn out and ill after his efforts in the eastern part of the empire. His capture of the Parthian capital, Ctesiphon, in the previous year had seemed to bring a successful close to a four-year campaign. Hadrian had been one of his trusted staff officers. For his efforts, Trajan had received the titles Imperator (conquering general) and Parthicus. However, this was the calm before the storm. The Roman Empire, larger than it had ever been before, was suffering strains. Trajan sacrificed to the ghost of Alexander the Great at Babylon before he heard that rebellions were breaking out in Cyprus, Egypt, and Libya, as well as in Dacia and Mesopotamia, where his recent successes had been achieved. The great warrior emperor, who had seen himself as a second Alexander the Great, must have been broken in spirit to hear that his new conquests were already causing such problems. He probably left Ctesiphon a bitter man.

Trajan knew he was ill. He had suffered a stroke and partial paralysis, but following the example of his hero, Alexander, he had chosen no clear successor. He had appointed Hadrian consul ordinarius, the top politician in Rome, for the following year, AD 118, but this in itself is no evidence that Trajan wanted him to become emperor. Trajan had said that he knew of many who could become the next emperor, but he had not taken the trouble to decide who this should be. Or so it seemed, until exactly one day after his death on August 8, AD 117. Then the news arrived in Syria that Trajan had in fact adopted Hadrian. It seems more than likely that the letter of adoption was written on the initiative of Trajan's wife, Plotina, who had always had a soft spot for Hadrian, either just before or just after the emperor breathed his last breath, and many saw Hadrian's new position as dubious at best.

On August 10, Hadrian had dreamt that he was touched by a fire from heaven but left unharmed, and then on the following day he received news of Trajan's death. This, at any rate, was his story, created perhaps to disguise the fact that Plotina and the new emperor had been in league over the whole sequence of events. It is impossible to be certain of this. Did Trajan really adopt Hadrian? Did Hadrian really have the dream? Whichever version of events is true, the new emperor's job was to convince the Senate, citizens, and soldiers of Rome that he was a worthy successor. But how had Hadrian ever gotten this far?

THE SPANISH BOY

Hadrian was born on January 24, AD 76, though whether he was born in Spain or in Rome is unclear. His father, Hadrianus Afer, was a senator and a praetor, a senior Roman official, who came from the Spanish town of Italica, now known as Santiponce, near Seville. His mother, Paulina, came from Gades, now known as Cadiz. The family was rich and important, with estates in Italica

A bust of Hadrian, sculpted sometime during or after his reign.

and Rome. Hadrian's father was the cousin of Trajan, who became emperor in AD 97. When Hadrianus Afer died, Hadrian was about ten years old, and Trajan became his guardian, along with another man, Publius Acilius Attianus. Hadrian may have spent some of his childhood in Rome and some of it in Spain. An early friendship was formed between Trajan's wife, Plotina, and Hadrian, who also got to know and admire Matidia, Trajan's niece. At the age of about fourteen, Hadrian put on a man's toga for the first time, an event that marked his new legal status as an adult, and he visited Italica to look over his estates. He now took an active part in the local association of wealthy young men, developing a keen interest in hunting.

Later, in AD 90, Hadrian came to Rome and was taken under Trajan's wing. He continued his education, and in AD 94 became a vigintivir (which literally means twenty-man), one of twenty officials in Rome chosen from the young nobles to serve for one year in minor official capacities. This was the first rung on the cursus honorum, the standard political career ladder, which was very well defined for the sons of upper-class Romans. In this capacity, he served in the courts as an attendant, learning the crafts of law and public speaking. He was also chosen to preside in the city during times of public holiday and celebration.

THE SOLDIER

Hadrian was selected in AD 95 to become a military tribune. This meant that he would be attached to a legion to assist in administrative duties and learn what it was to be a soldier. He went to serve in the second legion at Aquincum in Pannonia, on the river Danube, near modern-day Budapest. The second legion, called Adiutrix, had recently seen service in Britain, and it is tempting to think that Hadrian had conversations with soldiers even at that time about the northern frontiers of the Roman Empire. Hadrian went on to enjoy a second and even a third term as military tribune, with the fifth legion (Macedonia) in Oescus, in modern-day Bulgaria, and later with the twenty-second legion (Primigenia) in Moguntiacum, now called Mainz, in Germany. The hated emperor Domitian was killed in Rome in AD 96, and Nerva came to power. He in turn died in early AD 98, some time after adopting Trajan as his heir. Hadrian seized the opportunity to take news of the aged emperor's death to Trajan in Colonia Agrippinensius, now called Cologne.

Hadrian had a sister, Domitia Paulina, who had married an important Roman named Lucius Julius Servianus. Servianus was presently governor of Upper Germany, where Hadrian was tribune. Hadrian and Servianus seem not to have gotten along well at this time. Servianus is known to have complained to Trajan about the young man's extravagance and his excessive desire for hunting. At this stage it is likely that Trajan worried about Hadrian, since the young man had not yet earned his full confidence.

Trajan kept his position near the river Danube, keeping a watchful eye on the Sarmatian and Dacian tribes, who lived north of the river in modern-day Romania. Servianus became governor of Pannonia (modern-day Hungary), close to the river, which acted as a frontier at that time. In late AD 99, however, Trajan returned to Rome to become emperor, and among his followers was the young Hadrian.

A bust of Hadrian's wife, Sabina, who was introduced to him by Plotina, the wife of the emperor Trajan.

HADRIAN'S EARLY CAREER

Trajan and Hadrian had a quarrel at this time, which led to a cooling down between them. But in spite of their differences, the empress Plotina continued to support Hadrian, finding him a wife in AD 100, when he was twenty-four years old. Sabina Augusta was the daughter of Plotina's friend and the emperor's niece, Matidia, whom Trajan regarded almost as a daughter, so a close family link was preserved. Hadrian and Sabina may have started off well enough, but it is clear that their marriage was a convenience, and certainly in its later stages they were not fond of each other at all.

After this, Hadrian was elected to several positions that were steps up the cursus honorum. He first became a quaestor, or treasury official, in AD 101, which in turn meant that he could join the Senate. In this capacity, he occasionally stood in to read Trajan's speeches publicly and was made fun of for his strange accent in Latin. He may perhaps have had a slight Spanish twang to his speech. He

This carving from Trajan's Column in the center of Rome depicts Emperor Trajan commanding troops in the battle against the Dacians.

is known to have worked on improving this to reduce his embarrassment. Hadrian was often called "graeculus," or "little Greek," for his fascination with Greek language and literature. He was used to teasing, and strong enough to not show any discomfort over it.

Within several months of becoming quaestor, Hadrian was chosen by Trajan to join him as a

Roman soldiers are shown building fortifications on this carving from Trajan's Column.

member of his personal staff on the first expedition to Dacia. It was said that he became a drinking companion of the emperor to ingratiate himself with Trajan, learn his habits, and become closer to him. This campaign has been famously depicted on Trajan's Column in Rome. Roman legions marched into the area north of the river Danube in Romania to fight against the Dacian leader, Decebalus, who had been causing problems for some years. Within two years, Decebalus had surrendered to the Romans and peace was made, though unfortunately it would not last.

Hadrian was back in Rome by the next year, AD 102, and was made tribune of the people. At this time, his brother-in-law, Servianus, was con-sul, one of the two chief magistrates in the city, presumably keeping an eye on the young man's progress. Three years later, Hadrian became praetor, or senior magistrate. This meant that he was on a level with, say, a modern-day cabinet secretary or minister. War against Decebalus was declared again, however, since the Dacian king had not abided by his agreement after the first war. Hadrian once again went off to war with Trajan, this time in charge of the first legion, to serve in the second Dacian expedition, which finished a year later with the capture of Sarmizegethusa and the suicide of Decebalus. Trajan now added Dacia as a province to the Roman Empire along with Arabia, which had been acquired more peacefully.

In AD 107, Trajan staged a set of games in Rome to celebrate the success of the Dacian campaigns. Hadrian was decorated for his role in both cam-paigns, and he appears by this point to have earned considerable respect from Trajan and others, despite the earlier setbacks in their relationship. He was appointed governor of Pannonia Inferior and returned to Aquincum (modern-day Budapest), where he had been military tribune in his first term of office. This time, however, Hadrian was the man in charge, with absolute powers of life and death

King Decebalus of the Dacians commits suicide after his defeat by Hadrian.

over his subjects. A provincial governor had to ensure that Roman laws were upheld, that military matters ran smoothly, and that the finances were kept in order.

TRAJAN'S ADVISER

By early AD 108, Hadrian had become suffect consul, one of Rome's two senior magistrates. This was recognition from Trajan that his ward had made it to the top. Hadrian must have felt proud to have achieved this position at such a young age. He was only thirty-two. When he did return to Rome, he was given the job of writing speeches for Trajan and was certainly a member of the emperor's

inner group of friends. His various skills were also becoming apparent. Hadrian was an expert singer, a player of the kithara (a kind of early guitar), a poet, a philosopher, a military engineer, and an architect. He was also a keen painter and a sculptor. His interests were so diverse that he came into contact with many leading scholars, but this did not always make him friends.

An artist's reconstruction of the Forum Romanum, the political center of Rome, during the reign of Trajan.

The Roman economy was booming at this time, after the Dacian campaign had brought great wealth into the city. Apollodorus the architect was instrumental in building Trajan's famous markets alongside his new forum, and he did not want to see an amateur like Hadrian moving in on his territory, telling the young man to get back to his still-life sketches. One day the two argued while discussing Apollodorus's plans for the city and its port Ostia. Apollodorus felt confident in rejecting young Hadrian's advice, but it was an argument Hadrian never forgot.

After his consulship, Hadrian decided to embark on a tour that would take him away from Rome for the next eight years. He would not return until he himself had become emperor. As the former "graeculus," Hadrian wanted to see his beloved Greece, and his path took him first to Athens. Here he fit in so well with Athenian society that he was made an honorary Athenian citizen and even became the eponymous archon in the year AD 112. This meant that the Athenians had chosen him as their chief magistrate. This was of course only ceremonial, as Athens was by now just another part of the Roman Empire and not an independent state. It was at this time that Hadrian began to spread his influence in other ways, too. He grew a beard in the Greek style, which had not been commonplace among earlier Romans. Hadrian's beard would affect generations to come, creating a new fashion for his countrymen.

Some time after this, Trajan appeared in Athens on his way to the eastern empire and Parthia. Conflicts had broken out there that required his personal attention. Again he recruited his young adviser to follow him. The campaign brought the two men to Syria, Armenia, Mesopotamia, and even as far as Babylon, but this was the campaign that cost Trajan his life. Shortly before his death, Trajan had appointed Hadrian governor of Syria, and we return to the starting point of this story.

Officers and men of the Praetorian Guard, the special legion that protected the emperor, are depicted on this wall carving.

A NEW APPROACH

Once Hadrian came to power in AD 117, he had some serious difficulties to overcome before being accepted across the Roman Empire as the new ruler. The first of his troubles was the set of rumors that had arisen from the process by which he had gained power. It had been known for some time that Trajan had no heirs, so Hadrian's adoption just one day before the previous emperor's death looked at best suspicious and at worst downright dishonest. It was known that Trajan had promoted Hadrian and respected him but also that Empress Plotina had loved him as if he were her own son. It seemed that the new emperor owed his position more to her than to his "adopted father." Others said that Hadrian's former guardian Attianus was involved and that

Trajan had in fact died several days earlier, the news of the death kept quiet until Hadrian could be adopted.

Further problems faced the new emperor as a result of the general instability of the empire. Hadrian needed to take action quickly to restore order, as well as to make his own position secure. His first steps must have been seen as controversial. He proceeded immediately to abandon all Roman possessions in Mesopotamia, Assyria, and Armenia, thus undoing much of Trajan's recent work. All land gained in the region of the rivers Tigris and Euphrates was evacuated by the Romans, and it was not long before Hadrian also abandoned much of Dacia, captured in Trajan's two great campaigns, where he himself had played a role.

Hadrian sent a letter to the Senate in Rome, accompanying the old emperor's ashes, asking for the senators' pardon for assuming authority so soon and without their direct approval. At the same time, he requested that Trajan should receive divine honors and thus become a god in the Roman religion. Soon the reply came back that Hadrian's position as princeps, or first citizen, was approved. So his first worries were allayed, but there were still more concerns for the new ruler.

Within a short time, Hadrian dismissed Lusius Quietus from his job as governor of Judea. There may have been a number of reasons for this, but it is likely that Hadrian saw Quietus first and foremost as a rival for the imperial throne. By removing him from authority, he thought he was securing his own position. The Jews, however, saw this differently, thinking that Hadrian was protecting them from an anti-Semitic governor who had led the Roman assault against their rebellions in Cyprus, Egypt, and Libya. Quietus came from Mauretania (modern-day Morocco) in North Africa, and by his removal Hadrian caused civil disturbances to break out in that region. Hadrian ignored the advice of Attianus to put to death as pretenders to the throne Baebius Macer, prefect of Rome, and Calpurnius Crassus Frugi. Calpurnius was killed in any case some time later on Attianus's orders. At the same time, it was reported that there were uprisings in Britain. Hadrian was facing a bad time indeed.

DIVINE BEGINNINGS

Hadrian's skill at this stage of his career seems to have been in prioritizing tasks. He addressed each of his problems in turn, realizing that he could not do everything at once. Whereas he needed to do

Hadrian's Wall

BRITANNIA

GERMANIA

GAUL

PAN

Tibur
Roma
ITA

HISPANIA

SARDINIA

SICILIA

AFRICA

NUMIDIA

Boundaries of the Roman Empire ·····················

THE ROMAN EMPIRE AT THE TIME OF HADRIAN

DACIA

BLACK SEA

ARMENIA

MOESIA

PONTUS

PARTHIA

Byzantium

ASIA

PHRYGIA

MESOPOTAMIA

MACEDONIA

Ephesus

CILICIA

SYRIA

ACHAEA

Athenae

CYPRUS

JUDAEA

MEDITERRANEAN SEA

Alexandria

ARABIA

AEGYPTUS

River Nile

An amber colored glass jug from first-century Rome. Glassblowing had been invented in the first century BC.

some things in person, other situations could be trusted to colleagues. So he sent one of his most loyal, capable, and trusted friends, Marcius Turbo, to deal with affairs in Egypt and Libya. Turbo had been a centurion in Aquincum, and Hadrian had probably met him during his first posting there in AD 95. Hadrian himself, learning that the previous governor of Dacia had died recently, set off northward to go to this region. Before he left Syria, he stopped in a place called Daphne and took the strange step of blocking up a spring called the Castalian Spring, where apparently it had been foretold that he would be emperor. This was a symbolic act, as if to say that no other emperor would be proclaimed from that place, thus securing Hadrian's own position. Hadrian evidently could be very superstitious.

Hadrian's path took him from Syria to Ancyra, which is now part of modern-day Turkey. At

Ancyra, he allowed himself to be identified with the god of wine and was worshiped as the new Dionysus. This may have been the first time that Hadrian allowed himself to be called a god, but it certainly was not the last. It is interesting to speculate about how much the emperor himself may have believed in his own divine status. Certainly many of the people he ruled could be persuaded. If Hadrian could appear as a god in their eyes, he could gain greater authority with them. So we can see Hadrian's habit of allowing himself to be worshipped as part of his strategy to gain control over foreign peoples and achieve stability throughout the Roman Empire.

DIPLOMACY, DISASTER, AND CONSOLIDATION

On Hadrian's arrival in Dacia, he turned first to diplomacy rather than outright warfare, which had been Trajan's method of resolving things. The Roxolani tribe occupied lands to the north of the Danube in what is now Bulgaria. An agreement was made to split Trajan's newly acquired province so that the Roxolani tribe could become peaceful neighbors with the Romans. The king of the tribe was made an honorary Roman citizen to confirm the agreement. Dacia itself was divided into three

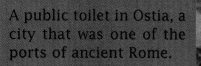

A public toilet in Ostia, a city that was one of the ports of ancient Rome.

separate Roman provinces, taking the place of the much larger administrative unit left by Trajan.

Meanwhile, in Rome, the absent Hadrian came under attack from his enemies, who saw his abandonment of Trajan's policies as disastrous for the future of the empire. It was becoming clear to them that the new man did not want to expand Rome's empire any further, and that his policies would favor strengthening what Rome already had rather than gaining any more land. Since the reign of Augustus, it was commonly believed by most Romans that the empire should continue to grow without bounds. Hadrian did not endorse this policy, creating conflict with several senior politicians. It was not long before they were voicing their objections.

Hadrian made his way to Byzantium, now the city of Istanbul in Turkey, where he spent some of the winter of AD 117–118 continuing to review his policies and preparing for a return journey to Rome, which he had last seen eight years before. Marcius Turbo, successful in his attempts to calm things down in Mauretania, was sent to Dacia as its new governor. This, too, must have irritated some career politicians, as Marcius had come to prominence as a soldier and had no political background at all.

Shortly afterward, disaster broke out in Italy when four men were killed, all of the highest rank in Roman society. They were ex-consuls, supposedly involved in a conspiracy against the emperor. One of them was Lusius Quietus, the former governor of Judea removed by Hadrian. He had a history of disagreement with emperors, having fallen out of Domitian's favor before his death. Also implicated were Avidius Nigrinus, who had been dismissed from Hadrian's personal staff, Cornelius Palma, and Publilius Celsus. It seems that the conspiracy, if it was indeed such, had been discussed in the Senate, which had voted to punish the four men. The punishment was carried out by Attianus, former guardian of Hadrian.

On his return to Rome, after the killing of the ex-consuls, the emperor tried hard to convince his subjects that he was no tyrant. Rome had seen several excessively cruel emperors, such as Caligula, Nero, and Domitian, and the people did not want to return to an age where the emperor's enemies mysteriously disappeared or were openly killed. Hadrian wanted to be seen as a man of the people, so he took steps to mix with them whenever he could. He did not use carriages when he could walk and did not stand on ceremony when it was unnecessary. He tried hard to distance himself from Attianus's actions and spoke about this in the Senate. Hadrian denied that the killings had been done on his orders and even dismissed Attianus as prefect of the guard in Rome, a post that was now taken by Hadrian's friend and loyal supporter Marcius Turbo. Turbo was to stay in this post for many years to come, and his continued presence in Rome protected the emperor's authority for almost all of his remaining time in power. As consul ordinarius himself for the first half of AD 118, Hadrian combined the role of princeps (emperor) with that of consul (prime minister), which was a fairly normal combination at that time. However, he gave up the post of suffect consul in July so that other consuls would be allowed to take up their posts, demonstrating his willingness to fit in with the standard practice of the time.

Hadrian now made a donation of six gold pieces to all Roman citizens, who had all previously received three gold pieces when he first came to the throne. This broad act of bribery of the people

This stone carving shows a Roman noblewoman at dinner. It was common for Romans to eat while reclining.

was an established way to gain popularity and was, Hadrian said, a way of sharing the success achieved in the provinces. Hadrian also pledged his ongoing support to the Senate and promised that he would never punish a senator without putting it first to a vote of his peers. He felt that the state, still referred to as the republic, should belong to its Senate and the people, and not be seen as the emperor's personal property.

Hadrian also canceled all previously existing tax debts going back as far as fifteen years. This was a popular move, as taxation in Rome was always problematic and at this time the money owed was a huge amount, around 900 million sesterces. Cancellation of debt on such a large scale left a massive sum of money available for spending, and Hadrian's measure boosted the Roman economy. Further steps taken by Hadrian included a reform of the law that said that the property of condemned people should go to the emperor's purse. Instead, it would now go to the public treasury. Payments to parents with children, introduced by Trajan, were raised to promote family life; parents now received financial support for girls to age fourteen and boys to age eighteen. Hadrian also made it illegal for masters to kill their slaves, which had previously been allowed by law.

As a result of his reforms, not to mention his wholesale bribery of the people, Hadrian was suddenly more popular than he had ever been before, and his abandonment of Trajan's policies was less resented. He was called the restorer and the enricher of Rome by people who only recently had called him a turncoat. The official deification of Trajan took place after his ashes had been installed in his column in the new forum. After this, a huge gladiatorial show was paid for by the emperor, in January AD 119. It was held to celebrate his forty-third birthday, and 1,000 animals were killed for the entertainment of the Roman people, including 200 lions.

This funding of public entertainment was an established way for an emperor or a leading politician to work up public support for his cause. Hadrian was consul ordinarius this year again, for the third and last time of his career.

Later in the same year, Hadrian went on a journey around southern Italy, spending time in the region of Campania, enjoying the pleasant climate, and visiting cities whose foundations dated back to Greek times. There does not seem to have been a motive for this trip besides the obvious one of taking a holiday. He was now much more at ease with himself and with his position, and he sought to maintain an illusion that he was just another citizen, though perhaps an elevated one. He was clearly a remarkable man, able to do many jobs at the same time, and apparently he had

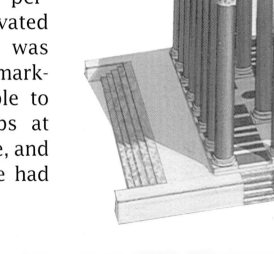

An artist's reconstruction of the Pantheon, with a portion of the exterior cut away to reveal the inside of the dome.

a phenomenal memory. It is said that he never forgot a name and could quote at length from the books he had read.

Toward the end of AD 119, Hadrian was upset to hear of the death of his mother-in-law, Matidia, who had been a good friend to him for many years. He allowed her to be deified. It is unknown whether Matidia had helped to keep relations good between Hadrian and his wife, Sabina, but his affection for the mother certainly seems to have been greater than that for her daughter.

Hadrian stayed in Rome for the next year or so, devoting much of his time and energy to internal politics and architecture, one of his favorite hobbies. It was at this time that he designed the Pantheon, one of the most beautiful buildings in Rome, still intact today. He set plans in motion to construct a huge temple for Rome and the goddess Venus near the forum, which would take many years to complete. Further projects included the strengthening of the river banks of the Tiber and the restoration of many buildings. Hadrian was modest about his accomplishments. Although it was customary for the person paying for a building to have his name inscribed on it, Hadrian's name appears on very few of the buildings he restored or built. Even the Pantheon did not have Hadrian's name written on it, though he totally redesigned and rebuilt the original construction, which had been erected by Agrippa in the time of Augustus.

As a symbol that he would no longer seek to extend the empire, Hadrian renewed the boundary stones of the city of Rome, which defined the city limits. In former times it had been customary to extend the boundary of Rome when the empire grew, so Hadrian was sending a clear message to his citizens, who had perhaps by now accepted the policy of nonexpansion, seduced by a series of populist policies. As part of Hadrian's propaganda for acceptance, he had coins minted that showed the new era as a golden age.

LIMITS OF EMPIRE

Hadrian stayed in Rome until April 21, AD 121, when a great festival was held in the city, perhaps designed as a grand send-off party for the emperor, who now chose to depart on his travels again. He had decided to survey the extent of his rule in the north and west of the empire. His journey took him through Gaul and Germany, and he inspected the military installations as he went.

The first major weakness he found in Rome's northern defenses was in the area between the Rhine and Danube Rivers in Germany. Hadrian was concerned that, wherever possible, natural features should be exploited and turned into barriers between Roman and non-Roman territory. So the huge rivers were important in delineating the frontiers of his rule. The Rhine, connecting the

North Sea to Switzerland in a long north-south line, formed one strong barrier, and the Danube performed a similar function along an east-west line stretching as far as the Black Sea. Hadrian had noted that the river Main, a tributary of the Rhine, was not being fully used and that the land lying between the Main and the Danube offered little protection against an enemy attack. This was where he first started to build an artificial frontier called a limes (pronounced lee-mez), the origin of the English word "limit." The German limes was a wall of wood, made of split wooden logs creating a palisade. It ran between Mainz and modern-day Regensburg.

A second weakness Hadrian noted was that the Roman army had now been at peace for so long in some of the frontier regions that it was losing its effectiveness and discipline. He insisted that rigorous training programs be introduced and adhered to, with soldiers practicing maneuvers, weapons training, and fitness regimes. Marches of twenty miles or more in full armor were carried out, and strict rules were established for soldiers or officers who wanted to go on leave. Clear age limits were established so that soldiers could not be too young or too old. Hadrian also instituted a policy for the legions that no money should be spent on equipment

An artist's reconstruction of the milecastle at Sewingshield, England. Milecastles were forts built along the length of Hadrian's Wall at intervals of a Roman mile, about 1,620 yards.

that was unserviceable. Hadrian maintained that there was no use having an army unless it was ready to defend the frontiers of the empire, and his reforms of military practice became standard for many years to come. In keeping with his man-of-the-people approach, he took an active part in these exercises, sharing quarters and food with his own soldiers.

THE WALL IN THE NORTH

After visiting Germany, Hadrian went to Britain in AD 122 with a newly appointed governor, Aulus Platorius Nepos. Hadrian aimed to secure a frontier system across the entire Roman world that would allow it to continue for the foreseeable future and beyond. But Britain did not really have an effective frontier system at all. Southern England had been occupied by the Romans in AD 43. Agricola had been governor of the province between AD 78 and AD 84, before being recalled to Rome by the emperor Domitian, and he had tried hard in that time to subdue the northern tribes, reaching as far as Scotland. There a battle was fought at Mons Graupius, the exact location of which is still a mystery. The outcome of the fighting was not clear, however, since Agricola's enemies kept making a series of guerrilla attacks on

The remains of Hadrian's Wall, west of Housesteads Fort, Northumberland, England, marking the furthest limit of Roman conquest in Britain.

the Roman troops. It was very hard for him to achieve any decisive success. Agricola decided to move south and consolidate a defensive system around two existing Roman roads, Dere Street and the Stanegate. The new northern frontier of the Roman Empire became a long, curving road, which did not create an adequate barrier between barbarians and Romans.

Hadrian's first concern was to strengthen the line of separation between Roman and non-Roman territory by constructing a long wall across the country. Unlike the limes in Germany, it was to be made mainly of stone, since this material was readily available in the region. The defensive system was to become Hadrian's Wall, a seventy-mile-long wall with extensive fortifications. The wall had one milecastle and two watchtowers for each mile of its length, with forts housing 500 or more soldiers spread out at roughly five-mile intervals. To the south, perhaps added after Hadrian's original plans were framed, there was a military road and a huge ditch-based system called the vallum, which created a kind of no-man's-land where only military personnel were allowed. The wall also had a ditch on the north side, which barbarians would have to climb through before being able to attack the Romans on the parapet, twenty feet above ground level.

Hadrian's Wall was and still is the largest construction project ever undertaken in Europe. Hadrian himself personally oversaw its design and the first part of the construction, resulting in the division between England and Scotland that remains today, although in the time that has passed the border has shifted many times from the line of his original wall. Its purpose was to separate the Romans from the non-Romans in Britain. So, like the limes, it both kept out the non-Romans and kept in the Roman citizens, providing a visible sign that Roman expansionism was over and that the existing empire should now be contained securely.

During his time in Britain, Hadrian came into conflict with some of his close colleagues, who apparently misbehaved in some way with his wife, Sabina. The details are not known for sure, but the historian Suetonius, who was also Hadrian's private secretary, was dismissed from his staff and sent back in disgrace to Rome, together with a senior officer called Septicius Clarus. Hadrian did not make many lasting friendships and had a habit of spying on his friends and colleagues. His relationship with his wife was almost certainly very poor by now, and he probably kept her with him on his travels for fear that she would do him harm if she was left

This carving depicts the tapping of a wine barrel in a tavern. Wine production was a major Roman industry.

alone in Rome. He once said he wished he could rid himself of her for being moody and difficult.

THE WESTERN EMPIRE

Toward the end of AD 122, Hadrian left Britain, bound for Gaul and Spain. It was on his way through Gaul that his beloved horse Borysthenes died and was buried in the south of France near Nimes. Hadrian also erected a temple there to Trajan's mother, Plotina, who had recently died. Hadrian wore black clothes for nine days to mark his grief for her. Hearing of a riot in Egypt, he addressed a letter to the people there that served to calm them down, and his journey continued. He spent the winter in Tarraco, in Spain, where he rebuilt the temple of Augustus. It was now that he began to simplify his own name to Hadrianus Augustus, and it is clear that he wanted to be seen as a second Augustus. Image was everything in the Roman world, just as now, and Hadrian sought identification with the first emperor of Rome, whose reputation remained unblemished.

This emperor, who traveled so widely in his life, made a curious omission from his trip to Spain. He failed to return to Italica, his own hometown. Whatever the reasons for this, he did donate generously to a building program in the town, which included a new amphitheater. Instead of visiting Italica, Hadrian went to Gades (Cadiz), his mother Paulina's hometown. During the trip to Spain, at some time in early 123, news arrived of a rebellion in Mauretania (modern-day Morocco), which Hadrian probably visited personally. Perhaps more seriously, problems resurfaced in Parthia. Hadrian now left his western empire to head east, where his rule had begun.

A TRIP TO THE EAST

By June 123 AD, Hadrian was back with his retinue of servants and followers in Antioch, Syria. He held a summit meeting in the area of the Euphrates with the Parthian king Chosroes and seems to have made a peaceful settlement. From here he went north to Cappadocia, where he visited another frontier system somewhat like the limes in Germany. He spent the winter in Nicomedia, in what is now northern Turkey. It was at this time that Hadrian met a young man called Antinous in the town of Bithynium Claudiopolis, which was to have momentous consequences later. Antinous at the time was about thirteen years old and may have been taken onto Hadrian's staff as a young retainer, accompanying him on his travels.

In the following year, AD 124, Hadrian moved through various parts of Asia Minor, going to the great cities of Ephesus and Smyrna. He called in at Rhodes, where he may have helped to restore the great Colossus, the wonder of the ancient world, a huge statue that towered over the harbor. Hadrian's habit was to create or promote a building project in the places he visited, something he could build or restore, demonstrating both his fascination with architecture and his passion for history—usually Greek. Another project supported by him on this trip was the completion of the Temple of Zeus at Cyzicus, begun 300 years earlier. Hadrian had the building completed and immodestly dedicated it jointly to Zeus and himself. He visited some famous monuments, such as the tomb of the famous Greek warrior Ajax at Troy, and on his travels he renamed many of the cities he visited either Hadriane or Hadrianopolis.

A painting of women performing rites associated with the Eleusinian Mysteries. This cult, which fascinated Hadrian, arose in ancient Greece, and its followers held celebrations every year in Athens.

Thus he made a mark wherever he went that was to endure for many years to come.

In the autumn of AD 124, Hadrian ended his eastern excursions with a second trip to Athens, where he realized a

long-held ambition of taking part in the Eleusinian Mysteries. Participants came from the entire Greek-speaking world, so Hadrian's involvement would not have been seen as exceptional, though it was clearly a very unusual thing for an emperor to do. These celebrations had been part of Athenian society for many years and were con- nected with the idea that wor- shipers experienced something that could assure them of life after death. The ritual involved a pro- cession of the people from Athens to Eleusis, about fifteen miles west of the city. The gods worshiped in the Mysteries were Dionysus and Ceres, mother of Persephone. Ceres, or Demeter as the Romans knew her, was the goddess of the crops and farming, whereas Dionysus, or Bacchus, was the god of wine. A swim in the sea for purification before the procession led to the torchlight ceremony. Full initiation did not come until a person had taken part in the Mysteries twice, so Hadrian must have had in mind even then that he would return.

Hadrian spent some time in the city of Athens and managed to create an extra tribe, named after himself. The tribes of Athens had been introduced about 600 years earlier as part of a political system for its general administration, and to enable voting to take place in manageable groups. Hadrian spent some time reforming the laws of this ancient and important city, which had influenced so many others and had always fascinated him. He then embarked on a brief tour of southern Greece, visiting Argos and Sparta among other cities. By March AD 125, he was back in Athens, presiding over the Great Dionysia, the most important of all the public festivals in the city. He now saw an opportunity to work on the largest of all the monuments he ever restored, the great Temple of Olympian Zeus at Athens. This great undertaking had been begun about 600 years before by the tyrant of Athens, Pisistratus, but it was still unfinished. Hadrian now resumed work on the buildings and started work on designs for the area around the temple, the temenos. At the same time, he began other building projects, including a new aqueduct for taking water from Mount Parnes to the center of the city. Near the agora, or city center, he also planned a library with a giant colonnade, called the Stoa.

After leaving Athens, Hadrian called in at Delphi, a world center for prophecy and the worship of Apollo. He tried to reform the body governing Delphi, the Amphictyonic Council. On his return to Rome, Hadrian stopped off in Sicily, where he energetically climbed to the top of the great volcano Mount Etna to witness the sunrise.

This mosaic from second-century Rome depicts gladiators in combat.

THE LAST GREAT JOURNEYS

CHAPTER 4

In spring AD 125, Hadrian was back in Rome. His travels had taken him around most of the empire and had lasted about four years. Now he needed to rest and take stock of what was going on in the capital of the empire. He had much to do, and he was not a man to stand still. He marked his arrival in Rome by having the gates of the Temple of Janus closed, a seldom-used sign that the Roman world was at peace.

Work on the Pantheon was now complete, but other building projects, such as the huge Temple of Rome and Venus, were still ongoing. Hadrian turned his mind to the restoration of the Temple of the Divine Vespasian and Titus in the Forum of Rome. In AD 126, Hadrian held office as a magistrate in Ostia, the nearby port of Rome, which was rather unusual.

Although serving emperors often held political posts such as the consulship in Rome, they seldom became involved in the politics of local communities outside the city. The emperor now devoted some attention to rebuilding the imperial palace on the Palatine Hill and to gaining more public support in Rome itself. A great set of gladiatorial games was held, where 1,835 pairs of fighters put on entertainment for the masses.

Hadrian spent some time out of the city at his estate in Tibur, modern-day Tivoli. Hadrian's Villa is a marvelous site to visit today, developed under the watchful eye of the emperor himself. Several buildings were named after sites in Greece, such as the Lyceum, Academy, and Poikile, and the villa also boasts a theater, a stadium, various temples, and libraries for both Greek and Latin books. A section of canal called the Canopus was developed, possibly after Hadrian's trip to Egypt in AD 130.

In early AD 127, Hadrian embarked on a tour of northern Italy, spending time in the valley of the river Po. He had divided Italy into four separate provinces, each having its own governor, but this was to prove unpopular and was abolished very soon after his death. He returned to Rome to celebrate the tenth anniversary of his accession to power in the summer of that year.

Hadrian's Villa, near modern-day Tivoli. The estate featured a theater, a stadium, temples, and libraries.

It was then that he allowed himself to be called "father of the country," marking a clear feeling of confidence in his own position and authority at this time.

AFRICA

In summer AD 128, Hadrian decided to visit Africa, which before this time had never enjoyed an emperor's personal inspection. By Africa, we mean the area of North Africa today occupied by Tunisia and Algeria. It is surprising that no emperor had been there before. Africa was closer to Rome than many other provinces and had been prosperous

The remains of an aqueduct built by Hadrian from Zaghouan to Carthage in North Africa

and peaceful since the destruction of Carthage in 146 BC. Perhaps because it was so prosperous and secure, visits by emperors before then had simply not been needed.

On Hadrian's arrival at Carthage, the local people were delighted that it rained, since it had

not done so for five years. This was seen as a good omen for the imperial visit. Hearing of the previous water shortage, Hadrian designed a new aqueduct running from the mountains at Zaghouan to Carthage. The old Punic city must have fascinated him, as did the ancient home of the legendary Queen Dido and the general Hannibal, who had caused such damage to Rome in the third century BC. Carthage had been razed to the ground and salt ploughed into the fields afterward, so crops would not grow there again. Then the region was left abandoned for about 100 years. After that, the Romans developed it, cutting the top off Byrsa Hill and establishing their own buildings on top of the Punic foundations.

In Africa, Hadrian carried out several important reforms that altered the status of existing settlements, so that it became easier for the inhabitants to acquire full Roman citizenship. Magistrates of municipia, or self-governing towns, had held this right before, but now it was extended to all town councilors. In addition, several towns that had been municipia were now changed to coloniae, meaning that all their inhabitants would automatically be Roman citizens and would therefore have improved legal rights, including the right to serve in a Roman legion. Hadrian also awarded ten native communities the status of municipium.

By June AD 128, Hadrian was on his way west to Numidia (modern-day Algeria), where the third legion (Augusta) was stationed at Lambaesis. The commander of the legion was Fabius Catullinus, who was to see the emperor inspect his troops most thoroughly. The army was required to construct certain stretches of limes frontier, though Hadrian again proved to be flexible as to the method of construction, this time deciding to use baked bricks of mud. The limes was used only to guard certain trade routes across the desert, and there was no apparent intention to create a continuous physical barrier across the province.

Hadrian approved of the generalship of Catullinus. He praised the soldiers for their building and their maneuvers, but he was critical of some of the cavalry tactics he saw being practiced. Clearly the emperor's praise was genuine, since Catullinus was later promoted to the office of consul in AD 130. Hadrian made his way west into Mauretania and sailed back to Rome from

Portus Magnus, on the coast of modern-day Algeria. His African trip had taken only a couple of months, and he was getting ready now for his last major visit to the eastern empire.

GREECE AND THE EAST

Since his visit four years earlier, Hadrian had wanted to return to Athens to take part in the Eleusinian Mysteries for a second time as a full initiate. He did this in September AD 128, on the first leg of his final excursion from Rome. This last trip was to take six years, leading to personal disaster for the wayfaring emperor. At its outset, however, he was clearly optimistic and looking forward to seeing some of his grander schemes come to fruition. Once again he was accompanied by his wife, Sabina, and a whole group of friends and companions. His grandnephew Pedanius Fuscus also joined the party, as the presumed heir to the throne.

Hadrian spent time at Athens and at Sparta, where he served as a local magistrate. He promoted membership in the Roman Senate among the Greeks, who had previously not aspired to this position, and he turned his thoughts again to forming a Panhellenion, a center for all things Greek, which he had been keen to create during his

This Roman mosaic illustrates a woman's initiation into the Eleusinian Mystery cult.

last visit to the country. This would take the form of both a building complex and a regularly held festival, which would be attended by Greek-speaking peoples in the same way that the Olympic Games were held. He saw the possibility of combining this with his plans to complete the sanctuary and Temple of Olympian Zeus at Athens, which he now made a priority. The area around the temple was called Hadrianopolis, and he himself took the extra name "the Olympian," both to show how serious he was about his plans and to identify himself with the chief god of the Greeks.

After spending the winter in Greece, he set out in early AD 129 for the eastern part of his empire, arriving in Ephesus, where his travels had brought him some five years earlier. He spent time here allocating funds to the Ephesians for dredging the estuary of the river Cayster, and then he moved off to see more great cities in the area. He traveled widely in what is now central Turkey, visiting among other places Phrygia, where he helped restore the tomb of the great Athenian leader Alcibiades, who had died there some 500 years earlier.

Hadrian's journeys had several purposes, though they no longer included the commitment to military consolidation that was apparent earlier in his career. He enjoyed hunting in Phrygia and shared this time with Antinous, his favored young attendant. He seems to have enjoyed the tour for its historical interest and to indulge his passion for all things Greek. In effect, Hadrian at this time was more of a tourist than an inspector of the empire.

However, there was always a political side to his activities, and one step Hadrian took was to consolidate his army and allocate sufficient numbers of coloniae around the empire so that the legions could be manned by locals where possible. Since the basic requirement for entry into the Roman army was that soldiers had to be citizens, it made sense to have at least one colonia near

A Roman mosaic depicting a number of hunting scenes. Hadrian hunted a lot during his last tour of the empire.

each legionary base, so that this condition could be satisfied. Hadrian is also known to have held another eastern summit meeting, perhaps in Syria, to discuss Parthia and Armenia. His efforts to secure an eastern peace by diplomacy rather than by force were ongoing from the earlier meeting with the Parthians held in AD 123, and he helped this one along by first releasing a hostage, the daughter of King Chosroes, as a gesture of good will. It was later said that Hadrian had achieved peace by bribing local chieftains, which may have been true. Hadrian introduced a policy whereby a local city acted within a region as a metropolis, or mother city. Antioch, Tyre, and Damascus were all given this title, which in practice does not seem to have meant much. Hadrian visited other places, including the beautiful city of Petra in the province of Arabia, which was given the name of Hadriane.

It was at the beginning of the next year, AD 130, that Hadrian began to involve himself in the problems of Judea, which had caused so much trouble for the Romans. There had been Jewish rebellions in Cyprus, Egypt, and Libya at the end of Trajan's rule, and since then the problems of the Jews had not been forgotten by the new emperor. As Hadrian approached Judea, he formulated new policies that were to create huge problems for him later on and fuel a full-scale rebellion in the province. First, there was the prohibition on circumcision, a practice that the Jews saw as fundamental to their religion. To the Romans, whose wish was to promote Greek habits and beliefs rather than Jewish ones, circumcision was abhorrent, and they saw it as a mutilation of the body. So it was banned, and the penalty for breaking the law was death. Hadrian also proclaimed that Jerusalem would be rebuilt now as a colonia of Rome, to be called Aelia Capitolina. Aelia was taken from Hadrian's own family name, and Capitolina from the name of the Capitoline Hill in Rome, the center of worship of the god Jupiter. It was to be built and guarded by the tenth legion (Fretensis), which had remained on site since the time of the emperor Titus and the sack of the city in AD 70. The Jewish holy city was therefore to become a center for the worship of Roman gods and the Roman emperor. There could have been no greater insult to the people of Israel, who began to hate Hadrian with a passion.

SORROWS IN EGYPT

Hadrian's travels in AD 130 took him on to Egypt, where he visited the tomb of Pompey the Great,

Caesar's great rival. Hadrian rebuilt the tomb and reerected a statue of the former statesman. Then he moved on to Alexandria, the city at the western Nile delta founded by Alexander the Great. Here he restored the Temple of Serapis, dedicating it in part to himself, as was now normal practice for him. This building had been damaged during the Jewish uprising in AD 116, so its repair was timely. Hadrian visited the Mouseion (museum), which was similar to a university, a center for artists, academics, and scientists set up by the great Macedonian king. As may be expected, Hadrian relished the contact with intellectuals of his age and entered into many debates where he enjoyed seeing his views prevail. Hadrian and his favorite Antinous enjoyed a lion hunt, perhaps their last occasion together in this capacity. Carvings depicting this event can still be seen in Rome, on the Arch of Constantine.

Hadrian next visited the town of Canopus, famous for its luxury and excess, and then he went on to Heliopolis (City of the Sun) where he saw the temple of the sun god and met a priest called Pancrates. This man may have had considerable influence on the emperor, who already had tendencies to believe in superstitions. Hadrian was shown books of spells and witnessed the magician priest conduct some bizarre rituals, supposedly causing people to have dreams, become sick, and die. Pancrates may well have accompanied Hadrian after this, as the emperor carried on southward up the river Nile.

It was on October 24, AD 130, that a horrible accident occurred that affected Hadrian very deeply. Antinous, his young attendant and homo-sexual lover, died while in the river Nile. How this happened is not clear. However, the date of the death was significant and may give cause for us to believe that this was no accident. October 24 marked the occasion when the Egyptian god Osiris had died, also in the Nile. Osiris was widely seen as ruler of the Underworld, someone who had returned to life after death. Furthermore, Osiris had been identified by some Greeks with Dionysus, a god whom Hadrian had been fasci-nated with for years. It was as the new Dionysus that Hadrian had first allowed himself to be wor-shiped in Ancyra all those years ago when he first became emperor, and he had been intrigued by the worship of Dionysus during his experiences at the Eleusinian Mysteries. It has been suggested that Hadrian was suffering ill health at this stage of his life and that Antinous may have been sac-rificed to bring him renewed health. It has also been suggested that Antinous committed suicide, perhaps influenced by what Pancrates or Hadrian

A bust of Antinous, Hadrian's young companion, dressed in an Egyptian costume.

wanted him to do. Whatever the truth, Hadrian would never be the same again and would always maintain that the death had been an accident.

The emperor now set about creating a new city to be called Antinoopolis (City of Antinous) at the site where his lover had died. Was the city built to commemorate the death, or was the death caused because the city was to be founded, to secure its future according to some superstitious belief? We cannot know the answer. However, despite Hadrian's state of mind—we are told he wept uncontrollably—he was on his travels again within a few days, arriving in Thebes by November 18, AD 130. The distance involved was about 250 miles, so Hadrian could not have stayed long to mourn at the site of Antinoopolis. The emperor said that he had seen a star of Antinous rise in the sky and this earned him some mockery.

On his arrival in Thebes, Hadrian wished to visit the so-called singing statue of Pharaoh Amenhotep III, which by some freak of nature caused a singing noise to be emitted at dawn as the sun's rays began to warm it. On the first day, the statue did not sing to the emperor, which was taken as a bad sign, but then on the second day, it did indeed perform. There is a great deal of super-stition in this, just as there is in so much else of Hadrian's reign.

Hadrian now returned to Antinoopolis, where he busied himself with the design of the new city. An obelisk was set up to Osiris and the newly dei-fied Antinous, called Osirantinous, in the hope that the emperor would live to an old age now that he was rejuvenated. This could be taken as evi-dence that Antinous did indeed die with Hadrian's full knowledge in some kind of magic pact. The worship of Antinous spread across the Roman Empire very quickly, extending to Greece, Asia Minor, and close to Rome itself, where a temple for Antinous was set up in Lanuvium in Latium. In April AD 131, a set of games was held in Antinoopolis, which Hadrian probably attended in person. A festival was held at much the same time in Alexandria to commemorate the death of Paulina, Hadrian's sister, who had also died recently. It was distasteful to many to see that

Hadrian's sister merited only a set of games, whereas his young lover had a complete city built as a memorial.

THE PANHELLENION

After this, Hadrian returned to Syria and Antioch, calling in at many other cities on the way. His route of travel is hard to identify exactly, but we know that he spent the winter in Athens, contributing further benefactions to the city. He held games in the stadium, where beast hunts were put on for the people's pleasure and 1,000 animals were slaughtered. The dedication of the shrine of Olympian Zeus was finally accomplished, and a huge statue of the god made of gold and ivory was uncovered. The Athenians, in recognition of the emperor's kindness, erected a statue of him behind the new temple. A gymnasium was opened near the city center, as was Hadrian's new library, with 100 columns of Libyan marble supporting it.

The Temple of Olympian Zeus was to act as the center for the new Panhellenion, the festival and focus for all things Greek. Hadrian wanted to hold the event every four years, and he also planned to use the new sanctuary for other large public events in the years between festivals. As a gesture of thanks to him, the people of Athens erected

A bronze gladiator's helmet. Gladiators were trained in schools for different kinds of combat. This helmet belonged to a retiarius, trained to fight with a trident and net.

Hadrian's Gate, an archway into the city bearing the inscription "This is the city of Hadrian, not Theseus." By late spring of AD 132, the tired emperor was ready to return to Rome, but events would not yet permit this to happen.

THE JEWISH REVOLT

News arrived in Athens of a rebellion in Judea, which gradually increased in its intensity. The causes of Jewish grievances have already been described, and soon the whole of Judea was in ferment. The leader of the revolt was one Bar Kokhba, or Bar Cocheba, also known as Shim'on. His name seems to have meant "son of a star," and he proclaimed himself as the prince of Israel. It is clear that he was hostile to both Romans and Christians.

Hadrian returned to the province to take care of things personally, but he also summoned his top general, Sextus Julius Severus, governor of Britain, to lead the Roman troops. In this extraordinary campaign, Hadrian achieved one of his most difficult and bloody conquests after three years of insurgency. The emperor returned to Rome for the last time, first taking a route northward to the river Danube, where he may have met to confer with Severus. Hadrian undertook a major drive to recruit more soldiers into the army from all across the

The Acropolis in Athens, with Hadrian's Gate at the foot of the hill.

empire to deal with the rebellion. Many people died on both sides of the conflict, with one source claiming over half a million Jewish deaths. Eventually, in AD 135, Bar Kokhba was killed, and his head was paraded in front of the Romans. Severus and his aide Publicius Marcellus were given triumphal honors in recognition of their success, an award rarely given to anyone other than the emperor. The ban on circumcision was not lifted and the new temple of Hadrian that arose in Aelia Capitolina remained a source of Jewish resentment.

HADRIAN'S LEGACY

Hadrian loved building things. On his return to Rome he worked on one of his last projects, his mausoleum. The first emperor, Augustus, had built a large, circular monument for himself in Rome, into which his ashes and the ashes of succeeding emperors had been put, up to and including the emperor Nerva. When Trajan died, it had been deemed proper to insert his ashes into his column. So now for the first time there was no obvious place for Hadrian's remains to be stored, unless, of course, he built one. Bearing in mind the size of the earlier emperor's resting place, Hadrian built a monument of almost exactly the same external dimensions on the opposite side of the river Tiber from the Mausoleum of Augustus. It was his last great building project. Leading across the Tiber to the mausoleum, now called the Castel Sant' Angelo, Hadrian built a bridge called the Aelian Bridge, now called the Ponte Sant' Angelo. The mausoleum and bridge lie just to the east of Vatican City.

There are many monuments built by Hadrian that still stand today. A visit to Rome should include a trip to the Pantheon, Hadrian's most beautiful building and the largest intact Roman building in the world. The great wall in northern England is another monument to this emperor's passion for building. All over the Roman world we can revisit Hadrian by looking at his monuments. The villa at Tivoli, which contains a number of replicas of monuments and buildings that the emperor had seen on his travels, including the Terrace of the Tempe and the Canopus, is a symbol of his devotion to architecture.

THE JOURNEYS

Hadrian's journeys are remarkable by anyone's standards, even today. He is known to have traveled in almost every province of the empire, a feat unequaled by any other emperor. Almost everywhere he went he either built something or held games. A basic outline of his journeys follows, with an estimate of approximate distances and dates.

HADRIAN'S TRAVELS

Year AD	Destination	Approximate Distance (in miles)
90	Italica	3,000
95–99	Aquincum, Moesia, Moguntiacum, Dacia	4,500
101	Dacia	3,000
105–108	Dacia, Pannonia	3,000
110–118	Athens, Parthia, Syria, Dacia, Byzantium, Pannonia	5,000
119	Campania	500
121–125	Gaul, Germany, Britain, Spain, Mauretania, Parthia	9,000
127	Northern Italy	500
128	Carthage, Numidia, Mauretania	3,000
128–134	Greece, Turkey, Syria, Arabia, Israel, Egypt, Dacia	8,500
Total Approximate Distance		**40,000**

THE MAN

Hadrian was tall, elegant, and had a full head of curly hair, with his Greek-style beard the most distinguishing of his features. He was highly intelligent and very well educated. He enjoyed debate with scholars from all walks of life, though he could not stand losing an argument. He numbered several philosophers among his friends, such as Epictetus and Heliodorus, though it seems that in old age he may have had less respect for intellectuals than when he was young. He claimed that he did not enjoy upsetting people in argument, which seems hard to believe. He once said that there was nothing in peace or war, imperial or private, that he did not know, and he obviously felt that mocking teachers of the arts was acceptable for a person of his wisdom. There are several stories that illustrate his arrogance. He argued with the architect Apollodorus, who disagreed with him on the design for the Temple of Rome and Venus, and he eventually had Apollodorus put to death. Favorinus, one of his philosopher comrades, once said he could not argue "with the lord of thirty legions." However, Hadrian did have a sense of humor, as the following exchange of poems shows. A poet called Florus wrote the lines:

I don't want to be Caesar
Walking around the Britons
Enduring Scythian frosts.

In reply, Hadrian sent him back the lines:

I don't want to be Florus
Walking around the pubs
Lurking among the sandwiches
Enduring fat mosquitoes.

The passion for all things Greek did not meet with universal approval among his Roman subjects. In his personal life, he met with problems from having intimate relationships with both men and married women, neither of which was acceptable to society in general. The emperor bore grudges and remembered arguments for years after they occurred. He was prone to allowing his friends to fall out of favor, and toward the end of his life he treated several old acquaintances particularly badly.

Hadrian was extremely hardworking and busy for most of his career, and like all busy people, he sometimes must have experienced great stress. A story was told of how a woman once met him and sought his help. "I don't have time," said the desperate Hadrian in his haste to

This Roman fresco, or wall painting, shows a gladiator fighting a lion.

leave. "Then stop being emperor," said the woman. Hadrian was at once brought back to his senses and returned to find out what the woman wanted. Hadrian's devotion to duty is also documented, and we hear of how he often interrogated prisoners in person, relying on

personal contact with witnesses rather than secondhand accounts.

Hadrian always walked around bareheaded, even in extreme cold and hot weather. He went to the public baths on many occasions, seeing this as an opportunity to mix with ordinary people. When organizing functions, he was often personally involved in the arrangements, and he would check the food destined for tables other than his own to ensure that the catering was not mishandled. He displayed courage on many occasions in his life, especially when he was once attacked by a slave in Spain. The slave of his host was carrying a sword and seems to have gone berserk, perhaps from a disturbed mind. Hadrian remained calm during this assault, disarmed the slave, and handed him over to the doctor for treatment. He was obviously a man who kept control of his physical and mental state, until in later life the strain became too great. He could also be ironic. Once a gray-haired man petitioned him for a favor, later returning with dyed, darker hair to repeat the request. Hadrian said, "I have already refused this request to your father."

An artist's reconstruction of the Basilica Ulpia, completed in AD 112, which flanked one side of Trajan's Forum. It was the largest basilica built in Rome up to that time.

The buildings he left behind were just part of his legacy, which extended across the Roman world. Hadrian made many social reforms, including those that secured the authority of the Senate and the safety of the people. In his reforms of the army, Hadrian created precedents for the empire that would last for many generations. His establishment of extra coloniae, providing a source of Roman citizens for recruitment into the armies, was crucial to the empire's later stability and allowed more people to become directly involved in government. Hadrian increased the rights of citizens in municipia, and this, too, promoted stability. In many ways he was an ideal emperor, because he cared about the long-term future of the Roman world. Yet it seems that his diffidence made it hard for people to like and trust him. He was always careful to ensure the loyalty of those around him, if necessary by spying on them and interrogating them in person. He was respected but not liked or trusted by many of those around him.

Hadrian's superstitious nature and his fascination with eastern religious cults may have brought him into conflict with traditional Roman beliefs, though he was always careful to adopt new faiths without compromising the old ones. However, his behavior in Egypt indicates that his judgment was clouded at this time by superstition, and his actions there cost him some support.

THE CRUEL CLOSE

After his final return to Rome, around AD 136, Hadrian's health started to deteriorate, probably as a result of a heart condition. He began to suffer from nosebleeds and other problems, and this made him turn his mind to who would succeed him. Some of his advisers considered the issue and Pedanius Fuscus, his sister Paulina's grandson, was their preferred choice. There was a disagreement among the advisers, however, and perhaps a plot. Fuscus was put to death. His grandfather Servianus, Hadrian's brother-in-law, now aged ninety, was encouraged to commit suicide for having supported Fuscus. This brought great shame and disrepute on the emperor, since old Servianus had served Rome loyally for many years and in many different conflicts.

Hadrian spoke of the advantages of adoption, saying that the selection of an heir by this method was preferable to passing on power to a natural son. However, he seems to have become suspicious of all those around him, and he began to detest many of his former friends. He appointed Lucius Ceionius Commodus his heir, calling him Aelius Caesar, but

A bust of Aurelius Antoninus, who became emperor upon Hadrian's death.

this man was already ill himself, vomiting blood regularly, and he died at the end of AD 137. At the same time, the empress Sabina died. We cannot imagine that her husband greatly mourned her passing. It has even been suggested that he poisoned her. At the beginning of AD 138, Hadrian announced publicly that he was ill and also that he had adopted Aurelius Antoninus as his successor. Taking an even longer view, Hadrian appointed two younger men to be next in line to the throne after Antoninus. They were Lucius Aurelius Commodus, son of Aelius Caesar, and Marcus Aurelius Verus, who later became the emperor Marcus Aurelius. Marcus had been a favorite of Hadrian for some time, and he was thought to have been preferred above all others by the emperor. It was probably just his youth that prevented him from being nominated first heir.

Hadrian had been cursed by old Servianus, who had wished him a dreadful death. The bitter curse now seemed to take effect. Hadrian wanted his life to end, but no one would help him. His doctors refused to administer a lethal drug and Mastor, his Hungarian master of the hunt, would not help him die either. His state of mind became more disturbed as he waited for death, and he removed from power Marcius Turbo, his most loyal of lieutenants and prefect of the city.

Hadrian embarked on a final journey from Rome to the Bay of Naples, where the mild climate would be less oppressive for him in his last days. He finally died on July 10, AD 138, cursing his doctors. We are told that he was hated by all at the time of his death, probably because both the beginning and the end of his reign were marred by the assassinations of popular public figures. He was deified by the Roman people only because the emperor Aurelius Antoninus, now known as Antoninus Pius, insisted on it. Hadrian wrote a poem shortly before he died, which he dedicated to his soul. It has been translated here as a fitting end to the story of his life.

> Small soul, wandering, sweet,
> Guest of the body, companion,
> Where will you go now? To places
> Pale, harsh, clouded,
> Nor, as you do normally, will you
>   make any jokes.

AFTER HADRIAN

Aurelius Antoninus became the next emperor after Hadrian. His rule is regarded as largely peaceful. At the outset of his reign he incurred criticism by insisting that Hadrian be deified, and it was this loyalty to his predecessor that gained him the name Antoninus Pius (meaning "pious," or "respectful"). There were few major wars in his reign, but campaigns in northern Britain led to the northward extension of the frontier from Hadrian's Wall and the establishment of the Antonine Wall. Antoninus Pius was popular, and the empire was perhaps at its most stable under

his leadership. He died in AD 161. He was suc-
ceeded by Lucius Aurelius Commodus. Lucius
died in AD 169 after ruling for nine years as joint
emperor with Marcus Aurelius. Hadrian had
required Antoninus Pius to adopt Lucius as third
in line to the throne in AD 138.

Marcus Aurelius Verus had an interest in phi-
losophy, which led him to write and publish a set of
meditations. During his reign, problems arose on
various frontiers, including Britain, Germany, and
in the eastern empire. A campaign north of the
Danube followed, and the Romans suffered a defeat
at the hands of the Marcomanni in AD 170. They

took vengeance on the Marcomanni two years later, and their victory was commemorated on the Column of Marcus Aurelius, or Colonna. The area north of the Danube was to cause more problems for Marcus Aurelius, and the emperor died there in AD 180, handing power over to his son Commodus.

HOW DO WE KNOW?

Primary sources for Hadrian are of two kinds. First, there is written evidence from two ancient biographies, that of Dio Cassius in Book 69 of his *Roman History*, and that given in *Historia Augusta*, a set of biographies written in the third century AD. Second, there is a wealth of archaeological evidence, in the city of Rome itself and all across the empire, in the form of buildings and monuments built by Hadrian. Hadrian's Wall in northern England is an exceptional site where one can see firsthand Hadrian's efforts to consolidate his empire.

GLOSSARY

colonia A Roman town or settlement, where all the inhabitants had the status of full Roman citizens.

consul The title given to a very senior Roman magistrate, a man who had reached the top of the cursus honorum. There were always two consuls chosen at any one time, in theory so that one could veto the other. A consul could serve for one year in his post and then often undertook a proconsulship, such as the governorship of a province, which could last for five more years. The emperor sometimes served as consul himself.

consul ordinarius This title was given to each of the two consuls whose term started off a new year.

cursus honorum Name given to the Roman political career ladder. A young man embarked on his cursus honorum by getting elected in sequence to a set of offices. This meant that he could become, in turn, vigintivir, military tribune, quaestor, aedile, praetor, and consul. In addition, he could become tribune of the plebs and serve in a variety of different priesthoods. After becoming quaestor, he was eligible to join the Senate, and if he achieved the highest positions of praetor or consul he would be qualified to serve as a provincial governor.

eponymous archon   A leading magistrate in Athens who presided over significant events, acting in the same sort of way as a leading town councilor or mayor. The eponymous archon was rather like a Roman consul ordinarius.

Imperator   Title given to a general who had been victorious in battle. It was often used as a term to indicate the emperor himself but had its origins in military life.

military tribune   "Tribune" was a term given to a variety of different officials in Roman society, simply meaning a magistrate, or official. A military tribune was usually a young man of senatorial background, chosen to serve for one year with the army, attached to a legion. His job was largely organizational, and in doing this job he would learn how the Roman army worked. Most unusual, the emperor Hadrian served as a military tribune on three different postings. Normally this would only happen once.

municipium   A town that had self-governing status, and whose officials became Roman citizens.

praetor   Title given to a senior Roman magistrate, a man who had almost reached the top of the cursus honorum. It is the equivalent in modern-day terms of a cabinet secretary. A praetor served for one year and then often undertook a propraetorship, such as the governorship of a province, which could last for five more years.

princeps Title given to the emperor. It meant "first citizen" and came into use at the time of Augustus, the first proper emperor of Rome. The princeps shared his authority with the Senate, though he was in effect the decision maker in most affairs.

quaestor Another official position for a young man making his way up the cursus honorum. A quaestor would serve for one year and have responsibilities for financial management within the Roman civil service. After serving in this capacity, a Roman nobleman would be eligible for election into the senate.

republic Term often used for the Roman state, represented by the acronym SPQR, meaning the Senate and People of Rome. Republic literally means "public thing."

Senate A body of about 600 senior statesmen, whose authority combined with the emperor's. The Senate acted as the lawgiver of Rome, and its importance in Roman history cannot be overestimated.

toga Woolen garment worn by Romans. A ceremony took place when a boy reached the age of around fourteen, when he put on a man's toga for the first time. This was a big event in a young person's life.

tribune of the people A term given to a variety of different officials in Roman society, simply meaning a magistrate, or official. A tribune of the people (tribunus plebis) was originally chosen to represent the people's interests against exploitation by the ruling classes. However, in imperial times the post had become much more of a formality and a tribune of the people would preside at public events.

vigintivir   One of twenty magistrates in Rome, usually picked from young noblemen embarking on their cursus honorum.

FOR MORE INFORMATION

ORGANIZATIONS
American Classical League
(National Junior Classical League)
Miami University
Oxford, OH 45056
(513) 529-7741
Web site: http://www.aclclassics.org
e-mail: info@aclclassics.org

American Philological Association
University of Pennsylvania
292 Logan Hall
249 South 36th Street
Philadelphia, PA 19104-6304
(215) 898-4975
Web site: http://www.apaclassics.org
e-mail: apaclassics@sas.upenn.edu

Classical Association of New England
Department of Classical Studies
Wellesley College
106 Central Street
Wellesley, MA 02481
Web site: http://www.wellesley.edu/
  ClassicalStudies/cane
e-mail: rstarr@wellesley.edu

WEB SITES

Due to the changing nature of Internet links, the Rosen Publishing Group, Inc., has developed an online list of Web sites related to the subject of this book. This site is updated regularly. Please use this link to access the list:

http://www.rosenlinks.com/lar/hadr/

FOR FURTHER READING

Baker, Rosalie, and Charles Baker. *Ancient Romans: Expanding the Classical Tradition*. New York: Oxford University Press, 1998.

Birley, Anthony R. *Hadrian, the Restless Emperor*. New York: Routledge, 1997.

Birley, Anthony R. *Lives of the Later Caesars*. New York: Viking, 1976.

Claridge, Amanda. *Rome: An Oxford Archaeological Guide*. New York: Oxford University Press, 1998.

Connolly, Peter, and Hazel Dodge. *The Ancient City: Life in Classical Athens and Rome*. New York: Oxford University Press, 1998.

Petren, Birgitta, and Elisabetta Putini. *Why Are You Calling Me a Barbarian?* Los Angeles: J. Paul Getty Museum, 1999.

Salway, Peter. *The Oxford Illustrated History of Roman Britain*. New York: Oxford University Press, 1993.

BIBLIOGRAPHY

PRIMARY SOURCES

Dio Cassius. *Roman History, Books 61 to 70*. Cambridge: Loeb Classical Library, 2000.

Dio Cassius. *Lives of the Later Caesars*. London: Penguin, 1976.

SECONDARY SOURCES

Boatwright, Mary Taliaferro. *Hadrian and the City of Rome*. Princeton, NJ: University Press, 1987.

Bowman, Alan, et al. *The Cambridge Ancient History, Volume XI*. Cambridge: Cambridge University Press, 2000.

Birley, Anthony R. *Hadrian, the Restless Emperor*. London: Routledge, 1997.

Claridge, Amanda. *Rome*. Oxford: Oxford University Press, 1998.

Lambert, Royston. *Beloved and God: The Story of Hadrian and Antinous*. London: Weidenfeld and Nicolson, 1984.

Perowne, Stewart. *Hadrian.* New York: W. W. Norton, 1962.

Many of these materials are available from the Teaching Materials and Resource Center of the American Classical League, Miami University, Oxford, OH 45056.

INDEX

ABOUT THE AUTHOR

Julian Morgan earned his B.A. in Greek studies at Bristol University, England, in 1979. He also earned a master's degree in computers and education at King's College, London, in 1990. He is currently head of classics at Derby Grammar School. Julian has a special interest in software design and has published many programs, including ROMANA and Rome the Eternal City, through his business, J-PROGS. He is a member of the American Classical League's Committee on Educational Computer Applications. He is the computing coordinator for the Joint Association of Classical Teaching (JACT) and has a regular column, "Computanda," in their bulletin. He also runs a training business called Medusa, which specializes in helping teachers of classics to use information technology in their teaching.

CREDITS

EDITOR
Jake Goldberg

LAYOUT
Geri Giordano

SERIES DESIGN
Evelyn Horovicz